Spark the Flame

By: Orlando Fernandez

Copyright © 2015 by Orlando Fernandez

All Rights Reserved.

The public is allowed to share any sentence of this book as long as: 1) it is done with Love, 2) financial gain is not involved, 3) the sentence is kept intact, and 4) credit is given to the title and author.

Original print and bind at the NYU bookstore:

726 Broadway, New York, N.Y. 10003

Original Edition

v1.1

ISBN: 978-1-939029-47-8

Library of Congress Control Number: 2015919620

Contact the author: o@sparktheflame.net

Thank you to my family, friends, and Life, all of who show me a healing Love and acceptance.

Table of Contents

Life is Yours 10

Using the Brain 24

Interconnectivity 34

Theory of General Positivity 40

Exponential Potential 62

Introduction

Spark the Flame

This book is made to inspire and to share patterns of Life observed.

Anything in here that is true you already know.

There is much said within the few words of this book.

Every sentence is valuable, please read accordingly.

Please reread to discover and internalize more.

You can randomly open a page to see what you find.

There is space to write your notes.

Love and Blessings.

Life is Yours

Life is Yours

I am an alcoholic.

I cannot control my drinking,

therefore, I cannot drink.

I wouldn't mind the lack of control,

except that it is harmful to me and

others.

Spark the Flame

I don't know what I will do later in the day, if I have a sip of beer at noontime for lunch.

That night, I might end up killing someone, accidentally or purposely, in a drunken stupor, possibly never remembering, and only realizing when I sober up.

Life is Yours

I share this because I have stopped

drinking now for three years, to

thank the divine Goodness of this

universe.

I had to, because I want to Live, and

while I was drinking, I was very close

to dying more times than I

remember.

It is up to me.

Spark the Flame

Because I take this difficult yet worthwhile path of sobriety for the sake and betterment of all, I earn assistance from Life to do good things here.

I give the sacrifice, I give the effort, I show Life that I am here to help.

And I believe.

Life is Yours

Whatever happens, I **believe** that

Life will help me to help the world.

I **believe** that I can.

I believe that **I can.**

I believe that I can.

Spark the Flame

Your Life has been entrusted to you.

You have a duty and blessing to

paint the tapestry of your story.

If you place this sacred responsibility

in the hands of another, choose

wisely.

Life is Yours

You are uniquely beautiful and valuable.

You have an exclusive Life path and Life pace.

You have your personal combinations of experiences, missions, needs, challenges, tendencies, preferences, skills, and energies.

Spark the Flame

Happiness is your choice, and when it occurs, it occurs Now.

If you are not going the direction you want, you must make changes to steer toward a different direction.

You are the one who must do it.

Life is Yours

Trusting yourself and trusting in Life,

you must do what you feel and know

is best in your heart.

Even when painful to yourself or

others, this will assure positive return.

Spark the Flame

If you believe, you **will** receive the

help you need.

It may come in unexpected space

and time, but it will show.

Life is Yours

Love is a journey.

Happiness, success, health, wealth:

they are not destinations.

They are all journeys.

They all begin Now, and

accompany you on the path.

Using the Brain

Using the Brain

Fill your mind and heart, action and being, with the Life you want to experience.

Spark the Flame

The more you repeat any thought, word, action, or feeling, the more likely you are to do so again, each time carving a deeper etching into your physical brain and human being.[1]

Using the Brain

To create a habit of something, practice it.

To break a habit, practice the opposite.

Practice who you want to be, and your brain will transform accordingly.

The brain works very mysteriously.[2]

Always, it connects with Life to produce circumstances that illustrate the person you are being.

For instance, when you deliberately continue the experience "I am blessed," your mind will produce surrounding conditions and personal perspective to confirm this.

Using the Brain

Sincerely repeat a list of gratitude multiple times daily, and you will soon find your list expanding.

Spark the Flame

Use your power of perspective to describe your Life as a beautiful story.

Using the Brain

Your choice and your gift is to custom-tailor your brain to create a world dear to your heart.

Interconnectivity

Interconnectivity

Everything is connected.[3]

Everything is part of a Whole.

Every portion of this universe

contains the whole universe.

Each moment, your thoughts, words,

actions and feelings affect everything,

everywhere, near and far.

Spark the Flame

We are like waves of the ocean.[4]

Connected to everything in the ocean, through the ocean, but also having distinctive shape and form.

The wave may crash and meld back into the larger ocean, but it can take shape and form again, all the while remaining ever connected and part of the all-encompassing ocean.

Interconnectivity

All things have equal inherent value.

Spark the Flame

The outside world is a reflection of

your inside world.

To create change on the outside,

make change on the inside.

Theory of General

Positivity

Theory of General Positivity

You are **already** Loved.

This can never stop.

The Whole is held together by Love.

You are a conscious conduit for this eternal Love, able to direct gushing currents toward wherever you wish.

Use your power of Love to

Love yourself.

Spark the Flame

Love All of yourself;

unconditionally, and without pretense.

Theory of General Positivity

Love yourself in the past, Love yourself in the present, and Love yourself in the future.

Love them **all.**

Fully, thoroughly and completely:

forever.

Spark the Flame

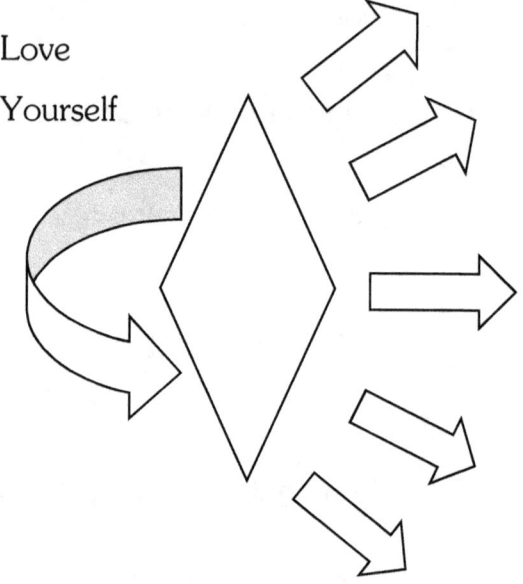

This Love is reflected
refracted to a Love of all

Theory of General Positivity

What is best for you and what is best for others is not mutually exclusive and is achieved through a unified harmony.

Faith converts adversity into

harmony.

Faith is the trust that when you aim

to do right, the best outcome for all,

Life evolves well for you.

Faith is the heart muscle of your

spiritual core.

This muscle is especially exercised

when you encounter adversity.

Theory of General Positivity

Based on your perception, things are either in process of working out for you or they are not.

When you hold the premise that things are working out for you no matter what is occurring in your Life, and you do all you can to aid that premise in thought and action, **this** is a Faith that converts adversity into harmony.

Spark the Flame

Regardless of how it appears from this vantage point, there is a great harmony to everything in existence.

Whenever you realize you do not have full control:

Trust in Life.

Theory of General Positivity

Sometimes it works transparently,

sometimes very mysteriously; but

given time, Faith **always** proves

itself.

Always.

Spark the Flame

You can **always** change your course and recover; this is human blessing.

The effort to recover from adversity and mistakes brings you growth and elicits assistance from Life.

Theory of General Positivity

Challenges will occur all your Life;

they serve as a way to grow.

If you are not growing, you are

dying.

For humans, stagnation devolves into

decay.

There are **always** ways to grow

and you must **always** exercise this

effort.

Spark the Flame

Self-honesty is imperative and must

be done with vigilance, forgiveness

and acceptance, and grit towards

mastery.

Self-honesty this way is self-healing.

Theory of General Positivity

Sincere, courageous effort opens

further paths to progress.

Spark the Flame

You are a piece of the puzzle that is

the Whole.

When you live abiding by the

uniqueness of your core, your

particular piece of the puzzle, you are

being authentic.

Theory of General Positivity

Authenticity is an endless journey of discovering yourself and sharing yourself.

You must unleash the freedom of expression that flows between your core and the rest of the world – the divine blueprint imprinted in your Soul.

Here you will find relief and sacred inspiration.

Spark the Flame

Authenticity frees your passion: unbridled Life energy that flows to you and through you because you have aligned so well with the great harmony.

You are literally living the part you were made for. The world **needs** your authenticity, and all are blessed when you embrace it.

Theory of General Positivity

Authentically fulfilling the role you are made for embodies connection with the Whole: forgiveness and acceptance.

The more you can forgive and accept yourself, the more you can forgive and accept others.

Forgiveness and acceptance are necessary for humanity to survive.

Spark the Flame

Life has **already** forgiven and accepted you.

To realize this is to heal.

When you heal yourself you heal the world.

Life forgives and accepts **all.**

Theory of General Positivity

The following is a quoted "loving kindness meditation":

If anyone has hurt me or harmed me knowingly or unknowingly in thought, word or deed, I freely forgive them.

And I too ask forgiveness if I have hurt anyone or harmed anyone knowingly or unknowingly in thought, word or deed.

Exponential

Potential

Exponential Potential

Life is ALIVE!

Sentient.

When you are on its team, you are

destined for success.

The cleaner your motives, the safer

you are.

Spark the Flame

Just like the human brain, our universe is mostly a mystery.[5]

The unknown harbors immeasurable potential and all unimagined possibility.

You must **believe** in this unknown.

Live the fact that anything and everything is possible.

Exponential Potential

Keep your destination in the forefront, and believe, and the path will be created: the road forming to meet each foot as it steps.

Spark the Flame

You can change your Life for the better at any point in time.

You can change Life on earth for the better at any time.

Every moment has a healthiest choice.

It is worth the effort to give your best.

Exponential Potential

The Flame is **you.**

And humanity.

Positive change engulfs the world as

you grow.

Spark the Flame

ARISE.

Fulfill your Loving purposes for the

better of all.

Spark the Flame

About the Author

I was born and raised in East Elmhurst, Queens, NYC.

I have a passion for writing and contributing positively to the world.

This is my first publishing; the contents having come through years of study, introspection, and observation.

I plan to publish further works on related topics.

Thank you for reading.

Notes

1. Doidge confirms in his preface: "a band of brilliant scientists...showed that the brain changed its very structure with each different activity it performed, perfecting its circuits so it was better suited to the task at hand...They began to call this fundamental brain property 'neuroplasticity.'" (Doidge xvii – xix).

2. Koch writes in essay *Project MindScope*: "The human brain, with its eighty-six billion nerve cells, is the most complex piece of organized matter in the known universe. It is the organ responsible for behavior, memory, and perception, including that most mysterious of all phenomena, consciousness." (Koch et al. 25).

3. Cox explains: "And so, every electron in the Universe knows about the state of every other electron. We need not stop there – protons and neutrons are fermions too, and so every proton knows about every other proton and every neutron knows about every other neutron. There is an intimacy between the particles that make up our Universe that extends across the entire Universe." (Cox and Forshaw 139).

Spark the Flame

4. The metaphor of everything connected as waves to an ocean has been used throughout the ages.

5. Tyson reports that mysterious dark matter and dark energy add up to **96%** of our universe: "From that we can then deduce how much ordinary matter, dark matter, and dark energy the universe comprises (the percentages are **4, 23,** and **73,** respectively)...cosmologists understand how the early universe behaved, but...most of the universe, then and now, consists of stuff they're clueless about." (Tyson and Goldsmith **61-62**).

Works Cited

Cox, Brian and Jeff Forshaw. *The Quantum Universe*. Boston: Da Capo Press, 2012. Print.

Doidge, Norman. Preface. *The Brain That Changes Itself*. Norman Doidge. New York: Viking Penguin, 2007. Print.

Koch, Christof, et al. "Project MindScope." *The Future of the Brain*. Ed. Gary Marcus and Jeremy Freeman. Princeton: Princeton University Press, 2015. 25. Print.

Tyson, Neil deGrasse and Donald Goldsmith. *Origins: Fourteen Billion Years of Cosmic Evolution.* 2005. New York: Norton, 2014. Print.

Spark the Flame

Physical Book Details

Dimensions:

4.25inches width by 7inches height.

Number of pages: 82.

Fonts used:

Oxford by Roger White

Book Antiqua

Gabriola

JasmineUPC

Elephant

Sow The Seed That Binds You

Feel The Steel That Signs You

Put Up All Your Resources

And Walk Into The Magic

—Zoraida Diaz